CATHOLIC UPDATE GUIDE TO THE
CATECHISM OF THE CATHOLIC CHURCH

Catholic Update
guide to the
Catechism of the Catholic Church

Mary Carol Kendzia,
Series Editor

Franciscan
MEDIA
Cincinnati, Ohio

RESCRIPT
In accord with the *Code of Canon Law*, I hereby grant my *Imprimatur*
the *Catholic Update Guide to the Catechism of the Catholic Church.*
Most Reverend Joseph R. Binzer
Vicar General and Auxiliary Bishop
of the Archdiocese of Cincinnati
Cincinnati, Ohio
August 30, 2012

The *Imprimatur* ("Permission to Publish") is a declaration that a book or pamphlet is considered to be free from doctrinal or moral error. It is not implied that those who have granted the *Imprimatur* agree with the contents, opinions or statements expressed.

Scripture passages have been taken from *New Revised Standard Version Bible*, copyright ©1989 by the Division of Christian Education of the National Council of the Churches of Christ in the U.S.A., and used by permission. All rights reserved.
Excerpts from the documents of Vatican II are adapted from the versions available at www.vatican.va.

Cover and book design by Mark Sullivan
Cover image © istockphoto | xyno

LIBRARY OF CONGRESS CATALOGING-IN-PUBLICATION DATA
Catholic update guide to the catechism of the Catholic Church / Mary Carol Kendzia, series editor.
p. cm.
Includes bibliographical references.
ISBN 978-1-61636-578-3 (alk. paper)
1. Catholic Church—Catechisms. 2. Catholic Church—Doctrines. I. Kendzia, Mary Carol.
BX1968.C385 2012
238'.2—dc23

2012033658

ISBN 978-1-61636-578-3

Copyright ©2012, Franciscan Media. All rights reserved.
Published by Franciscan Media
28 W. Liberty St.
Cincinnati, OH 45202
www.FranciscanMedia.org

Printed in the United States of America.
Printed on acid-free paper.
12 13 14 15 16   5 4 3 2 1

Contents

About This Series vii

Introduction ix

Chapter One
What Is the *Catechism of the Catholic Church*? 1

Chapter Two
A Walk Through the *Catechism* 11

Chapter Three
The Four Pillars: Creed, Sacraments, Morality, Prayer 17

Chapter Four
A Quick Look at the U.S. *Catechism* 33

Conclusion 43

Sources 47

Contributors 49

About This Series

The Catholic Update guides take the best material from our bestselling newsletters and videos to bring you up-to-the-minute resources for your faith. Topically arranged for these books, the words you'll find in these pages are the same clear, concise, authoritative information you've come to expect from the nation's most trusted faith formation series. Plus, we've designed this series with a practical focus—giving the "what," "why," and "how to" for the people in the pews.

The series takes the topics most relevant to parish life—e.g., the Mass, sacraments, Scripture, the liturgical year—and draws them out in a fresh and straightforward way. The books can be read by individuals or used in a study group. They are an invaluable resource for sacramental preparation, RCIA participants, faith formation, and liturgical ministry training, and are a great tool for everyday Catholics who want to brush up on the basics.

The content for the series comes from noted authors such as Thomas Richstatter, O.F.M., Lawrence Mick, Leonard Foley, O.F.M., Carol Luebering, William H. Shannon, and others. Their theology and approach is grounded in Catholic practice and tradition, while mindful of current Church practice and teaching. We blend each author's style and approach into a voice that is clear, unified, and eminently readable.

Enrich your knowledge and practice of the Catholic faith with the helpful topics in the Catholic Update Guide series.

Mary Carol Kendzia
Series Editor

Introduction

"So what's the difference between the *Catechism of the Catholic Church* and the Bible?" No, this isn't a hypothetical question to set up a definition of the *Catechism*. It's an actual question asked by someone presumably educated in the Catholic faith and working in a Catholic environment.

It has been fifty years since Vatican II, thirty years since Pope John Paul II called for a new comprehensive summary of Catholic doctrine, and twenty years since the document was completed. Still, a significant number of people are unaware that it even exists, let alone are familiar with its contents. And yet, broadly speaking, the *Catechism* simply articulates and elaborates what we say every Sunday in the Creed, the way we strive to live morally and ethically, and the way we communicate with God in prayer.

The most sacred book in our tradition is the Bible, the story of God's relationship with humankind from the beginning of creation through the full revelation of the divine self in Jesus and the promise of his presence for all time in and through the life of the Church. Much of the content of the *Catechism* includes quotes and citations from the Scriptures.

The word *catechism* opens up many windows of memory for Catholics who lived in the pre–Vatican II Church. It was common practice to memorize the questions and answers found in the *Baltimore Catechism*; this practice was considered the bedrock of religious education.

That method was great for discipline and a wonderful way of developing the memory; but precious little intelligible catechesis —faith education—took place. And it is hard to buy the argument that, even though you did not understand it then, it would become clear later. Today, our understanding of religious instruction is that it has to reach a person where he or she is now or it is not authentic catechesis.

Fortunately, the new *Catechism of the Catholic Church* is not intended to develop our memories. (Such an approach would pose a formidable task indeed, since the *Catechism* runs to 904 pages!) Rather, it is a gift from the teaching authorities of the Church (the magisterium) to the faithful in order that they may more fully understand the riches of the salvation God has offered to us in Jesus Christ.

On the thirtieth anniversary of the Second Vatican Council, Blessed Pope John Paul II included this declaration in the formal document that ordered the publication of the *Catechism of the Catholic Church*:

> I declare [the *Catechism of the Catholic Church*] to be a sure norm for teaching the faith and thus a valid and legitimate instrument for ecclesial communion. May it serve the renewal to which the Holy Spirit ceaselessly calls the Church of God, the Body of Christ, on her pilgrimage to the undiminished light of the Kingdom!

CHAPTER ONE

What Is the Catechism of the Catholic Church?

For Catholics of a certain age, the word *catechism* summons memories of questions and memorized answers. But the term has another meaning: a comprehensive, systematic presentation of the truths of Catholicism. The Church has published two such catechisms in her history.

The first one was the catechism of the Council of Trent, or the *Roman Catechism,* issued in 1566. Enormously influential, this catechism went through 817 editions in four centuries. Cardinal Newman loved it: "I rarely preach a sermon, but I go to this beautiful and complete catechism to get both my matter and my doctrine." Pope John XXIII was still recommending it in 1960.

The second comprehensive, systematic catechism was published in 1992 and is the focus of this book. Called the *Catechism of the Catholic Church,* it is the result of seven years of effort dating from the 1985 synod of bishops that requested it. Pope John Paul II formally issued it on December 8, 1992.

Why was a new catechism needed? Many new issues have arisen since 1566, such as ecumenism, the revised liturgy, new social problems, and new moral issues, such as those caused by test-tube babies and atomic warfare. A second reason is the need to address "contemporary consciousness" which deals with problems in personal and historical terms. A third reason is to take into account the new pastoral awareness awakened by Vatican II, especially in its document *Gaudium et Spes* (The Church in the Modern World).

The *Catechism of the Catholic Church* belongs to a unique literary form. A catechism is a book of unchallenged answers. Even when a catechism follows the question-answer format so familiar to many from the *Baltimore Catechism* (the *Catechism of the Catholic Church* does not), the answers, not the experience of people, dictate what the questions will be. A catechism poses a built-in danger of giving the reader a kind of smug sense of being "right." One might mistakenly think there is no need for the student or teacher to struggle with the questions, as they would in other areas of study, because the answers are all there. There are no debates to be engaged in, for there are never two sides to an issue.

Certain and *beyond challenge* written clear over every page: This is what gives a catechism its unique flavor and identity. A book characterized by such unyielding confidence can be a help for Catholics. In a world filled with all sorts of uncertainties, it can be a comfort to have the security of a catechism. On the other hand, this inflexible air of confidence can also pose a problem. Life continually poses new questions—questions that never occurred to the writers. How are Catholics to deal with such questions? Will a closed-minded mentality, which the catechism may tend to encourage in some people, leave them unprepared to face the unexpected question?

This is not to say that one cannot take the light of faith gained from a catechism and use it to shed light on new situations and problems. The questions still remain, however: Does our experience of these new situations and problems in any way illuminate the truths of faith? Do they help us to see aspects of those truths we never saw before? Do new questions and situations stretch our minds and deepen our understanding of what God is trying to teach us?

A Very Brief History of Catechisms

The first catechisms (somewhat like the Gospels) were spoken before they were written. They began as instructions given to the newly baptized by such Fathers of the Church as Cyril of Jerusalem or John Chrysostom of Constantinople, and later were committed to writing. Later catechisms (such as the Council of Trent's *Roman Catechism* and the United States bishops' *Baltimore Catechism*) reversed this process. They were written first and then became the source from which catechists drew to give instructions to children, young people, and interested adults.

In other words, in the beginning catechesis came first, rising out of the experience of the catechist and the community; only later was it put into a written document or "catechism." Later catechisms, on the other hand, were written first out of the experience of the Church, then used by catechists. What should be clear is that, whether catechesis or catechism comes first, the key to effective catechizing is the catechist.

How the *Catechism* Came to Be

On January 25, 1985, Pope John Paul II called an extraordinary assembly of the Synod of Bishops to commemorate the twentieth anniversary of the Second Vatican Council. At this meeting, it was proposed that a catechism—or compendium of Catholic doctrine on faith and morals—be composed to serve as a sourcebook for local catechisms to be written in countries around the world.

In 1986 the pope appointed a commission of twelve bishops to carry out the task of drawing up such a sourcebook under the leadership of Cardinal Joseph Ratzinger (now Pope Benedict

XVI), head of the Congregation for the Doctrine of the Faith. The commission was made up of experienced and distinguished Church leaders representing Europe (both eastern and western), the United States, South America, Africa, and the Eastern Catholic Churches of the Middle East. Two Americans were on the commission: Cardinal William Baum of Washington, D.C., and Cardinal Bernard Law of Boston.

The task of the commission was to work out the general structure and character of the catechism. It also followed the text as it gradually took shape through nine successive drafts. These drafts were created by an editorial board of seven bishops from Spain, France, Italy, England, the United States (Archbishop William Levada of Portland, Oregon) Lebanon, and Austria. Bishop Christoph Schönborn of Austria acted as intermediary between the commission and the editorial committee.

A first draft was completed in the spring of 1988. This text was written in Latin and translated into various languages. In November 1989 this first draft, called the *Catechism for the Universal Church,* was sent to all the bishops for their suggestions and criticisms.

What resulted was a first-rate exercise of collegiality. The recommendations sent in by the bishops around the world were given serious consideration, and significant changes were made in succeeding drafts. The Commission for the Catechism and its editorial committee completed their work on February 14,

1992. The ninth and last draft bore a different name: *Catechism of the Catholic Church.* This normative text, from which all translations are made, was written in French, and Pope John Paul II approved it on June 25, 1992.

In the Vatican Palace, on December 10, 1992, while the Sistine Choir sang Palestrina's Mass in honor of the Blessed Virgin Mary, Pope John Paul II gave the new *Catechism* to the world.

Goals of the *Catechism*

The *Catechism* is a sourcebook that surely and authentically articulates the teachings of the Catholic Church. Its primary intent is to inform. A person who reads it should have, at the end of the reading, a reasonably clear understanding of what is officially taught by the Church.

Yet sensitive readers will face an immediate problem. Having read such a huge amount of material, they will instinctively realize that all of it cannot be of equal importance. How, they will want to know, can we discover some way of distinguishing what is of primary importance from what is of secondary importance?

The *Catechism* quotes a statement from Vatican II to make it easier for us to strike a balance between what we need to be ready to die for and what is of lesser importance: "There exists an order or 'hierarchy' of truths, since they vary in their connection with the foundation of the Christian faith" (Decree on Ecumenism, 11).

This text is helpful; still, it creates a problem of its own: Neither the Council nor the *Catechism* defines the "foundation of Christian faith." It seems important to make an attempt to identify it.

Several answers are possible. We can safely say that the foundation of the Christian faith is the resurrection of Jesus. Most likely, this is what Pope Paul VI means when he said in his 1975 encyclical, *Evangelization in the Modern World*: "Evangelization will always contain—as the foundation, center, and at the same time, summit of its dynamism—a clear proclamation that, in Jesus Christ, the Son of God, made man, who died and rose from the dead, salvation is offered to all men as a gift of God's grace and mercy" (27). Much closer in time to the foundation reality itself are the words of Pope Paul's namesake, who said that "if Christ has not been raised, your faith is futile and you are still in your sins" (1 Corinthians 15:17).

This position fits with what the *Catechism* says: "The Resurrection of Jesus is the crowning truth of our faith in Christ, a faith believed and lived as central truth by the first Christian community; handed on as *fundamental* by Tradition, established by the documents of the New Testament; and preached, as an essential part of the Paschal Mystery, along with the cross" (638; emphasis added).

From this foundation flow baptism, which incorporates us into Jesus's death and resurrection, and the Eucharist, which celebrates those events. Baptism and Eucharist give birth to the Church. Members of this Church are linked to one another in a communion called to promote justice, goodness, and peace.

One could go on and on, showing how the beliefs we ascribe to, the moral commitments we strive to follow, and the spirituality we try to live can be traced back to the Resurrection as the foundation of Christian faith. This is offered as a possible unifying truth with which to approach the material in the *Catechism*. Other truths might also be chosen as foundational: for example, our belief in a Trinitarian God, or our belief in the unconditional love of Jesus, and his command that we imitate that love.

If the *Catechism*'s primary goal is to offer a good bit of information about Catholic beliefs, its second goal, rivaling the first in importance, is to offer a strong challenge to those whose privileged responsibility it is to teach the Catholic faith. It calls them to foster and deepen the faith life of the Church community by focusing on doctrinal, moral, and spiritual content as the base on which to build true Christian community.

The Authority of the *Catechism*

While the Holy Father described the *Catechism* as "a sure norm for teaching the faith," it is important for us to realize as we read it that the statements it makes do not all have the same authority or importance. Statements from the councils of the Church have the highest authority, since they come from the highest teaching body in the Church—the pope and bishops gathered together in solemn assembly. Statements from the individual Fathers of the Church or from various theologians have whatever authority these statements possessed before they were included in the *Catechism*.

This is not just an opinion; it is the position taken by the man whom Pope John Paul II charged to bring the *Catechism* to completion, Cardinal Joseph Ratzinger. In a seminar held on July 9, 1993, in Madrid, Cardinal Ratzinger said, "Every doctrinal point proposed by the *Catechism* has no authority but that which it already possesses."

The cardinal makes a very important point that we must keep in mind when reading the *Catechism*: It is not inclusion in this book that gives authority to a particular statement. Rather, as the cardinal makes clear, whatever authority they have belonged to them before they were inserted in to the *Catechism*. Understanding this principle will help us see that not everything in the *Catechism* is of equal authority or importance. Catechists, especially, need to keep this in mind when they use it as a reference work.

Questions for Reflection

1. How familiar are you with the *Catechism of the Catholic Church*? What more would you like to learn about it?
2. "Neither the Council nor the *Catechism* defines the 'foundation of Christian faith.'" Do you agree that the foundation of the Christian faith is the resurrection of Jesus? If not, what do you see as the foundation of the faith?
3. What has been the primary way you have learned the truths of the faith?

CHAPTER TWO

A Walk Through the Catechism

What is the big picture of the *Catechism of the Catholic Church*? Think of a triangle with the words *revelation*, *faith*, and *magisterium* at each point. Here is a catechism that describes a dialogue between a God-revealing and a faith-responding people in the environment of the teaching of a Spirit-guided Church (magisterium).

This vision is spelled out successively in four pillars: (1) the creed—the faith professed; (2) the sacraments—the faith celebrated; (3) morality—the faith lived; and (4) prayer—the faith deepened.

Behind the triangle and the pillars is a unifying flow. In other words, there is a natural flow or progression from the teachings of God's revelation of salvation found in the creed into the sacraments, into Christian moral and social witness, which is reinforced by prayer. The believer's faith response to the Trinity of Persons is a constant theme throughout. So also is the work of the Spirit.

The tone of the *Catechism* is positive and non-polemical. The mood is confident, reflecting the abundance of graces and teachings available to Catholics from the generosity of God. Each teaching emerges in a milieu of Scripture, Tradition, Church history, council statements, liturgical citations from both the Eastern and Western Catholic churches, and quotes from the saints and the Fathers of the Church.

How is the *Catechism* meant to be used? (1) Diocesan bishops use it to sponsor and encourage the writing of other catechism and religion textbooks adapted for various age groups and the cultural needs of the local Church. (2) Homilists benefit from it for their ministry of the word. (3) The general Catholic reader can use it as a reference for growing in a spiritual, doctrinal, and moral understanding of Church practice and teaching.

The *Catechism* builds upon the traditional teachings of the Church and incorporates the insights of Vatican II and other major documents published since that council. In fact, four-fifths of all the quotes from Church councils are from Vatican II.

The *Catechism of the Catholic Church* follows the traditional outline of a catechism. Like the *Roman Catechism* of the Council of Trent, it is divided into four parts: creed, sacraments, commandments, and prayer.

A charming feature of the *Catechism* is that color photographs of artworks introduce each part and suggest its basic theme. Part one (the creed) features a fragment of a fresco from the catacombs of Priscilla in Rome—the most ancient image of the Virgin Mary in existence. She is pictured holding her son and with a star over her head. At her left is a prophet, probably Balaam, announcing "a star shall come out of Jacob" (Numbers 24:17). The image introduces the central theme of the creed: the incarnate Son of God, born of the Virgin and given to all humankind.

Part one begins with a section on revelation, the initiative whereby God addresses people, and on faith, humanity's response to that revelation (26–184)

Part two (liturgy and the sacraments) is introduced by a fresco from the Church of Sts. Marcellinus and Peter in Rome. It depicts Jesus's meeting with the woman who for many years had suffered from hemorrhage (see Mark 5:25–34). The woman is touching the hem of Jesus's cloak. Jesus's hand is extended toward her as he realizes that power has gone out from him. What the photograph says is that the sacraments are visible signs of the saving and healing power of Jesus that come forth now from the Risen One present among us.

Part two has a section on liturgy (1066–1209), which introduces the discussion of the seven sacraments. Liturgy is seen as revelation, communication, and acknowledgment of the blessings God has visited on humankind. These blessings are proclaimed in Scripture from "the liturgical poem of the first creation" (Genesis) to the "songs of the heavenly Jerusalem" (Revelation).

The section on the commandments (part three) offers the central section of a Roman sarcophagus dating from the year 539. Christ is portrayed in glory. The apostles Peter and Paul receive from him two scrolls, representing the twofold Great Commandment: love of God and love of neighbor.

Part three, which deals with the Ten Commandments, is introduced with a long section on the Christian way (1691–2051). It is made up of three chapters. Chapter one, "The Dignity of the Human Person" deals with such topics as the image of God, human happiness, freedom, the morality of human acts, moral conscience and sin. Chapter two, "The Human Community," discusses the person and community, participation in social life, social justice, and human solidarity. Chapter three, "God's Salvation: Law and Grace" includes such topics as the moral law, the new law of the gospel, grace and justification, and the Church as mother and teacher.

Part four ("Prayer and the Our Father") opens with a colored miniature from Mount Athos in Greece. It depicts a desert scene.

Jesus is absorbed in prayer to God the Father, who appears in the upper right-hand corner. The disciples are there, too, but they stand in awe at a respectful distance. Only after Jesus has finished his prayer do they make their request: "Lord, teach us to pray" (see Luke 11:1).

Part four, on prayer, has no special introduction, although its first section, "Prayer in the Christian Life" (2558–2758), prepares for a study of the Lord's Prayer (2759–2865). Many aspects of prayer are discussed: prayer in the Scriptures and in the life of the Church, the sources of prayer, the way people have prayed, different schools of prayer, and the role of prayer in the family.

Questions for Reflection

1. In what ways is the *Catechism* helpful to you?
2. How do the four sections of the *Catechism* relate to one another?
3. How do these four "pillars" of the *Catechism* relate to your own life of faith?

CHAPTER THREE

The Four Pillars: Creed, Sacraments, Morality, Prayer

The wealth of material in the *Catechism* is not adequately conveyed by its fourfold division. Each of these divisions has an important introductory section that puts its topic in context.

Revelation and Faith

The section on the Creed begins with this fundamental teaching that will ground the rest of the *Catechism*. Religion begins with God's revelation of his loving, creative, and redeeming work. Our response is a Spirit-inspired and Spirit-guided faith. This response is both personal (I believe) and communal (we believe). Our growth in faith is a lifelong process. The teaching office of the pope and bishops (the magisterium), guided and protected by the Spirit, oversees the faith message and fosters this divine/human dialogue.

A Trinity of Persons. Reason can know the existence of God as an impersonal force or higher power. Only revelation can disclose that God is personal, living, and forgiving, three persons in one divine reality or nature: Father, Son, and Spirit. "Even when he reveals himself, God remains a mystery beyond words…" (230).

Our Father. God is Father as creator of the world. Yet, "…[He] is Father not only in being Creator; he is eternally Father by his relationship to his only Son who, reciprocally, is Son only in relationship to his Father" (240).

God created us in his image. This means that only humans are able to know and love God and share in his life. Our souls most clearly reflect the image God. Our bodies also reflect the image God by becoming temples of the Holy Spirit. God created us male and female to be a communion of persons in marriage and to procreate human life.

The fall. Scripture says we started out as friends of God in paradise, but were tempted by the Evil One to abuse our freedom and seek fulfillment outside of God. "Adam and Eve transmitted to their descendants human nature wounded by their own first sin and hence deprived of original holiness and justice; this deprivation is called 'original sin'" (417). God did not abandon us. From the beginning, God promised us a savior. The Son of God fulfilled that promise of salvation.

God the Son. The church believes that the center and purpose of all human history is found in Jesus Christ, her Lord and master. The name Jesus means "savior." The name Christ means "anointed one," or Messiah. Jesus is the Son of God. He has a unique and eternal relationship to God his Father. He is the only Son of the Father (John 1:14,18). God "adopts" the rest of us. "To be a Christian, one must believe that Jesus Christ is the Son of God…" (454).

Jesus is also the son of the Virgin Mary. In our profession of faith we pray: "by the power of the Holy Spirit he was incarnate of the Virgin Mary and became man." The Church confesses that Mary is truly 'Mother of God' (*Theotokos*)" (495). We believe Jesus possesses two natures, divine and human, united in the person of the Son of God.

The redemption. Jesus redeemed us from sin through his life, death, and resurrection. Here the *Catechism* quotes John Paul II:

> The whole of Christ's life was a continual teaching: his silences, his miracles, his gestures, his prayer, his love for people, his special affection for the little and the poor, his acceptance of the total sacrifice on the Cross for the redemption of the world, and his Resurrection are the actualization of his word and the fulfillment of Revelation. (561)

"Christ died for our sins in accordance with the Scriptures…" (1 Corinthians 15:3). Christ's death and resurrection were necessary for our salvation. The liturgy of the Eastern Church sings "Since it brings life, the tomb of Jesus is lovelier than paradise. It is the fountain from which our resurrection springs." Paul says that Easter is essential for our faith. "If Christ has not been raised, then empty is our preaching, empty, too, your faith" (1 Corinthians 15:14).

God the Holy Spirit. The Holy Spirit is God, the third person of the Blessed Trinity. Because the Holy Spirit is a divine mystery, many images are needed to perceive this divine person's reality and sanctifying action. Scripture links the Spirit with the waters of baptism, the oil of anointing in confirmation, the fire of religious enthusiasm, the shining cloud and fire of God's glory-presence, the seal of salvation, the hand of God's protection, the finger of exorcism driving evil from us, and the dove of peace (see 394–701).

Jesus promised us the gift of the Spirit. "I will send him to you…. He will guide you to all truth" (John 16:7,13). Jesus conferred the Holy Spirit on the apostles on Easter night (John 20) and on Mary, the apostles, and the disciples at Pentecost (Acts 2). The work of the Spirit is irrevocably tied to the Church.

The Church. At Pentecost the Holy Spirit brings the Church into the world. The Church embraces the kingdom already inherited but not yet completed. The Church is a mystery, a communion, and an institution.

In the first place, the Church is a mystery because she has a divine founder. God the Father intended the existence of the Church as a sacrament, meaning a sign and cause of salvation. The Son of God, Jesus Christ, instituted the Church, "for it was from the side of Christ as he slept the sleep of death on the Cross, that there came forth the 'wondrous sacrament of the whole Church'" (Constitution on the Sacred Liturgy, 5, quoted in *CCC,* 766). This emphasis on the Church as sacrament was stressed at Vatican II. God the Holy Spirit visibly revealed the church at Pentecost.

Second, the Church is a communion of people summoned by God to listen to his word with faith, actively participate in worship, and form covenant with him and each other (see *CCC,* 777).

Third, the Church is an institution. From New Testament times onward the Church community was guided by the Spirit to assure its stability and continuity. In the New Testament itself we see a progress from the simple community life described in the Acts of the Apostles to the growth of structures in the pastoral epistles of Timothy and Titus. The seeds of the Church's hierarchical life are already evident in the later passages of the New Testament and are fixed in the early part of the second century.

Fourth, the Church, as servant, works for the well-being of the human and social order. The extensive social teachings of the popes from Leo XIII to John Paul II are evidence of this, and the *Catechism* stresses it in 1928–1948.

Mary and the last things. The *Catechism* focuses on the traditional Marian doctrines: Mary's perpetual virginity, her motherhood of God, her immaculate conception, and her assumption. It also speaks of her as Mother of the Church, our chief model of faith, and our principal intercessor in heaven. Whatever is taught about Mary is always in reference to Christ and the mystery of salvation. "What the Catholic faith believes about Mary is based on what it believes about Christ, and what it teaches about Mary illumines in turn its faith in Christ" (487).

Mary is interested in our life here and our final destiny hereafter. In all things, we are urged to look to the final purpose and destiny of our lives—the last things: death, judgment, purgatory, heaven, hell, the immortality of the soul, the resurrection of the body, and the end of the world. The *Catechism* takes up these teachings in 988–1065.

Mary, the Mother of the Church, walks with us on this final journey. The Holy Spirit is our interior power and strength for achieving this goal through imitation of and union with Christ, through active faith, sincere participation in the sacraments, and a Christian witness in the personal and social orders.

Liturgy and Sacraments

The liturgy of the Catholic Church celebrates the presence of Christ in his Church here and now—in the community of his people, in his ministers, in his word proclaimed, and especially in the Eucharistic bread and wine. Liturgy is the action of the Holy Spirit, "the Church's living memory" (1099), who makes present among us the mystery of Christ.

In the liturgy, the Church celebrates the paschal mystery by which Jesus accomplishes the work of salvation within us. The words *paschal mystery* refer to the saving life, death, and resurrection of Jesus. In Galilee and Jerusalem, Jesus performed the work of salvation once and for all. The Holy Spirit makes this saving work of Jesus present to us in the liturgy of word and sacrament.

The seven sacraments are seven forms of celebration.

> It is the whole community, the Body of Christ united with its head, that celebrates. "Liturgical services are not private functions but are celebrations of the Church which is 'the sacrament of unity,' namely, 'the holy people united and organized under the authority of the bishops.' Therefore liturgical services pertain to the whole Body of the Church. They manifest it, and have effects upon it. But they touch individual members of the Church in different ways, depending on their orders,

their role in the liturgical services, and their actual participation in them" [Liturgy, 26] (1140).

Lay participation and ministry in liturgy are encouraged, again demonstrating how the Catechism reflects Vatican II.

What are sacraments?

The sacraments are efficacious signs of grace, instituted by Christ and entrusted to the Church, by which divine life is dispensed to us. The visible rites by which the sacraments are celebrated signify and make present the graces proper to each sacrament. They bear fruit in those who receive them with the required dispositions. (1131).

As we shall see in the following sections, sacraments are grouped according to initiation, reconciliation, and ministry.

Sacraments of Initiation. Baptism, confirmation, and Eucharist are the sacraments of initiation into the Christian life. Baptism initiates us into the life of the Spirit, union with Jesus, and membership in the Church. In describing the sacrament of confirmation, the *Catechism* quotes Vatican II's document on the Church: "For 'by the sacrament of Confirmation, [the baptized] are more perfectly bound to the Church and are enriched with a special strength of the Holy Spirit. Hence they are, as true witnesses of Christ, more strictly obliged to spread and defend the faith by word and deed'" (1285). The Eucharist completes the process of Christian initiation. The Rite of Christian Initiation of Adults (RCIA), an important practice reinstated after Vatican II, is described in the *Catechism*, 1229–1245.

The Eucharist is the sacrificial meal of salvation and it contains the entire treasure of the Church—Jesus Christ. The *Catechism* (1328–1332) lists nine names for the Eucharist which, taken together and essentially connected, give us some sense of the full meaning of this sacrament. The names for this sacrament are: Supper of the Lord, Eucharist, Breaking of the Bread, Eucharistic Assembly, Memorial, Holy Sacrifice, Holy and Divine Liturgy, Communion, and Holy Mass.

Sacraments of healing. Reconciliation and the anointing of the sick are the sacraments of healing. The sacrament of penance and reconciliation (also sometimes called confession), through the forgiveness of sins, reconciles us to God, the Church community, and to ourselves. The anointing of the gravely ill unites their sufferings to the cross, grants forgiveness of sins, and prepares them for passage to eternal life with the Risen Christ.

Sacraments of ministry. Holy orders and matrimony are sacraments of ministry, meaning they serve salvation. Matrimony calls the spouses to minster to their mutual salvation and that of their children and families. "Unity, indissolubility, and openness to fertility are essential to marriage" (1664).

Through Holy Orders, the ordained are called to serve the salvation of the priesthood of all believers. The three degrees of the sacrament of holy orders are deacon, priest, and bishop. Both matrimony and holy orders are directed to the salvation of others.

Christian Morality

The *Catechism* entitles this section "Life in the Spirit," thus showing a positive, grace-filled vision of and approach to our moral lives. Beginning with Christ's laws of love of God, others, and self, the text deals with our human dignity as images of God, our freedom, and our call to holiness. It explains the morality of human acts and passions, outlines virtues that should be acquired to stay moral, and teaches us how to form our consciences.

The formation of conscience includes responsiveness to the inner working of the Spirit, natural law, the revealed commandments, the teachings of Jesus, and the teachings of the magisterium. A treatment of the meaning of sin follows this section.

The next step is a meditation on the human community, the demands of social justice and peace, and the Church's social teachings. It makes clear that our moral life should be both personal and social. A social conscience is essential to moral living. Here again we see a new emphasis coming of age in recent decades.

The final section deals with the Ten Commandments. The first three are grouped under the heading of "love of God." The final seven are treated under "love of neighbor." "The first and last point of reference of this catechesis will always be Jesus Christ himself, who is 'the way, and the truth and the life'" (1698).

Continuing its positive approach, the *Catechism* says that morality is a response to God's love. Christian morality also includes:

a resolve to do God's will
admission of the existence of sin
an emphasis on grace and the call to holiness
the practice of lifelong moral conversion.

The *Catechism* places the presentation of the Ten Commandments in the context of Christ's twofold command of love: love of God, subject of the first three, and love of neighbor, the concern of the remaining seven (2052–2055). Thus the commandments, which include a number of "thou shalt nots," are cast in a more positive context. While in no way mitigating the importance of the things we need to avoid (murder, adultery, stealing, and so on), the *Catechism* offers love as the motive that should prompt our avoidance.

The *Catechism* also prepares us to study the commandments by speaking about general issues involving our moral life: the actions of persons involved in keeping the commands of love. In 1691–2051 it speaks about the communities to which we belong and in which we exercise responsibility. It discusses the morality of human actions, the meaning of conscience, virtue, and vice. It clarifies the new law of the Gospel and the role of the Church in teaching about moral matters. By the time it begins its discussion of the commandments, we have the necessary moral equipment at hand to deal with the issues raised by them.

Prayer

Our prayer will make our faith in the creed stronger, our fidelity to the sacraments mightier, and our moral life more profound. Prayer is the soul of the *Catechism*. Prayer is religion's special language. At a level deeper than intercessory prayer, human beings experience the need to relate to the One who brought them into existence. One way they seek that relationship is prayer (2566–2567).

Life is a journey from God, who is our beginning. We journey also toward God, who is our destiny. Yet it would be a mistake to think that God only shows up at the beginning and the end, with perhaps an occasional appearance in between. No, we travel toward God *with* God: We are always in a relationship of intimacy with God. But more than that, we travel *in* God. We are in communion with God, which is to say that, though distinct from God, we are never separated from God. For separation from God would not mean merely that we would cease to journey; we would cease to exist.

To say that we travel toward God with God and in God is to make clear that prayer is not first a human initiative, but a divine one. On life's journey, it is God who first calls us. Tirelessly God invites us to that mysterious encounter that we have come to call prayer. In the words of the *Catechism*: "Whether we realize it or not, prayer is the encounter of God's thirst with ours" (2560). What a fascinating experience it is when we do realize it!

Prayer is a many-faceted reality. The *Catechism* points to various aspects of prayer by leading us briefly through the Old Testament, the New Testament, and the story of the Church.

A description of the expressions of prayer—vocal prayer, meditation, mental prayer (including contemplation)—serves as a prelude to a discussion of common struggles in prayer and the need to persevere in a spirit of love.

All this is preliminary to the climax toward which the *Catechism* is leading: the study of the prayer most cherished by Christians, the Lord's Prayer, which the second-century writer Tertullian called a "summary of the Gospel."

The *Catechism* concludes with a meditation on the seven petitions of the Our Father (see 2759–2865). The Lord's Prayer is a beautiful gift that Jesus has given us. It is the first gift the Church gives to catechumens as they prepare for the sacraments of initiation. Born anew in the living waters of baptism, catechumens learn to invoke their Father by the Word God always hears. Most of the commentaries on the Lord's Prayer written by the Church Fathers—and there are many—are addressed to catechumens or to the newly baptized for this reason. The Lord's Prayer is the prayer of the Church *par excellence*. An integral part of the Divine Office (also referred to as the Liturgy of the Hours), it also has a place of prominence in the Eucharist, coming between the Eucharistic Prayer and Communion.

Though we often say the Lord's Prayer privately, it is first and foremost the prayer of the Christian community. The *Catechism* quotes St. John Chrysostom as saying that the Lord teaches us to pray for our brothers and sisters in community by inviting us to say not "*my* Father who art in heaven" but "*our* Father" (2768). Praying the Our Father helps protect us against a narrow individualism. It reminds us that this prayer is the heritage of all the baptized.

Prayer is the power of the heart. The spirit of the *Catechism* is prayerful from page one to the end. For those who plan to study the *Catechism*, whether in full or in part, a prayerful attitude is the best way to do so. Then God will be praised and our hearts will be full.

Questions for Reflection

1. What role does the Church play in God's revelation?
2. What significance do the sacraments have in your spiritual life?
3. Reflect on the *Catechism*'s teaching that morality flows from the Great Commandment—love of God, self, and neighbor. What practical meaning does this have for you?
4. What are the obstacles to prayer in your life?

CHAPTER FOUR

A Quick Look at the U.S. Catechism

After the *Catechism of the Catholic Church* was published, the United States bishop conference approved a document called the *United States Catholic Catechism for Adults*. The purpose of this book is to give Catholics in the U.S. a unique look at the history of the Church from the founding of this country forward. Like the *Catechism of the Catholic Church*, it is a catechetical tool meant to encourage a deeper understanding and practice of the faith—in this case, from the perspective of life in the United States and the development of the Church in that context.

Pope John Paul II said of the *Catechism of the Catholic Church*: "It is meant to encourage and assist in the writing of new local catechisms, which take into account various situations and cultures, while carefully preserving the unity of faith and fidelity to Catholic doctrine."

Therefore, the original intent of the *Catechism* was to help diocesan bishops, bishops' conferences, and catechism writers draw up new local catechisms. These would provide an opportunity to take cultural differences into consideration and, at the same time, preserve the unity of the Church's faith. The prologue to the *Catechism*, while preserving the original intent, also suggests that the *Catechism* will be a help to catechists and useful reading for all the faithful.

The fact that the English translation of the *Catechism* hit the bestseller list soon after publication indicated that it was reaching a wider audience than the one envisioned by the pope and the commission who drew up the document. Such success prompts the question: Was it necessary to develop a catechism for the U.S.? Yet the authors of the *Catechism* make clear that local catechisms are indispensable because of the need to adapt doctrinal content and catechetical methods to the differences in culture, age, spiritual growth, and social and ecclesial conditions that exist among the people of God.

Why the U.S. Needs Its Own Catechism

No self-respecting teacher uses an encyclopedia as a basic text. True educators draw from life, connect to truth, and point toward contemporary circumstance and culture. In religious education, the work of meditation and prayer completes the circle of engagement. While this seems to be a universal truth, it poses particular challenges.

Catholics of different nations or regions face varied circumstances, are engaged by examples drawn from their experience, and live their faith within a culture shaped by history, geography, and economics into a particular flavor—and it's never vanilla. An adult primer of faith must respect and engage its readers by recognizing and respecting that God-given variety. Pope John Paul II saw the need for this and the bishops of the United States responded.

Big Picture of a Big Book

Any Catholic who has consulted the 904-page *Catechism of the Catholic Church* also knows the general outline of its U.S. counterpart. Just as was true in the *Baltimore Catechism*, the creed, sacraments, commandments, and prayer are the structural and thematic pillars of this new book.

Both books carry a positive, confident tone and are rooted in Scripture. Both include summary statements highlighting doctrinal emphases. Given these parallels of approach and structure, what makes the *U.S. Catechism* distinct?

Three elements deserve special note: (1) stories; (2) application to American culture; and (3) inclusion of meditations and prayers.

Stories

The preface and the next thirty-five chapters begin with a story (the final chapter [36] begins with a summary of Gospel teaching on prayer.) These brief biographies include saints and near saints, laymen and laywomen, religious, priests, bishops, a cardinal, and two popes. Native American, black, Canadian, Puerto Rican, and Hispanic persons are represented.

Some of these holy people are well-known to most Catholics, others less so. The closer they are to grassroots America, the more edifying is their effect. Each story has a logical link to the chapter that follows. Here's a sampling of the holy U.S. Catholics one can meet in the *Catechism*—some, perhaps, for the very first time!

Women founders of religious communities: The intrepid pioneer spirit of the six sister-founders who introduce various chapters is inspiring. Elizabeth Ann Seton, Mother Frances Cabrini, Rose Hawthorne Lathrop, and Katharine Drexel are perhaps better known but these women are no more courageous than Henriette Delille, who challenged Catholics to overcome prejudice, and Mother Joseph, honored in Washington, D.C.'s Statuary Hall. Sister Thea Bowman was not a founder in her own right, but perhaps is best placed together with these women, given her prophetic voice for black Catholics in the Church.

Lay leaders: Dorothy Day and César Chávez were champions of social justice and have long been heroes to many Catholics, but you may not be familiar with journalists Orestes Brownson and John Boyle O'Reilly or lay apostle Carlos Manuel Rodriguez of Puerto Rico. Pierre Toussaint and Kateri Tekakwitha may have ministered more quietly, but they nevertheless led by example. Catherine de Hueck Doherty, though not a U.S. citizen, profoundly influenced many Americans through the houses devoted to the lay apostolate she and her husband founded throughout the world.

The ordained: The rest of the U.S. Catholics profiled in the *Catechism* include eight priests (sometimes two to a chapter), three bishops, and Cardinal Joseph Bernardin, whose example in facing death fittingly introduces the chapter on the sacrament of the anointing of the sick.

Doctrine Applied to Cultural Challenges

The themes of human dignity, fairness, respect, solidarity, and justice are among those treated. As the *U.S. Catechism's* introduction states, sometimes this application is positive, but it may also address difficulties such as subjectivism, relativism, and moral decision-making dilemmas.

Granted that people of every culture around the globe face crises of faith, these crises will be spawned and fostered within a culture. It takes glasses adjusted to that cultural perspective to see them clearly for what they are. The catechism issued by the Vatican could not possibly go in enough detail to address such local variety!

The *U.S. Catechism* takes on the critical issues of American culture and demonstrates clearly how the faith of old applies to these new challenges and situations.

Prayer

The *Catechism of the Catholic Church* says, "Prayer is the life of the new heart. It ought to animate us at every moment" (2697). The *U.S. Catechism* honors that "ought" by concluding each chapter with an appropriate meditation, prayer, and Scripture citation. Some are from the holy person whose story opened the chapter. Many are spiritual classics. The invitation these elements present reminds students of the catechism the reason for their reading: to love God and to prepare for service of God.

The *U.S. Catechism* also includes an appendix of traditional Catholic prayers. Since chapter thirty-five says, "The will to pray in a daily, sustained, and structured manner is essential for becoming a prayerful person," the long-revered texts of tradition make excellent starters.

How the Text Teaches

The U.S. text is three hundred pages shorter than its Vatican counterpart. The U.S. volume includes several elements (described earlier) that the international text does not. One can only conclude that when some things were added, others were left out or condensed. Does this imply that the teaching of the universal *Catechism* was altered or deleted? Not at all!

***This book does not replace the* Catechism of the Catholic Church.** Both books are foundational. The constant references to the Vatican text within the *U.S. Catechism* remind readers that the two volumes are partners.

Since the newer book is especially designed for American Catholics, it forms an excellent bridge for connecting to the earlier, larger (and, let's face it, more difficult and scholarly) book when the U.S. text awakens a hunger, inspires a question, or creates a need to know more.

This book is directed to a specific audience (young adult Catholics) but keeps the entire U.S. Roman Catholic (and Eastern Catholic) community in mind. The *U.S. Catechism* is simpler in structure, content, and language than its international "elder" volume. That's a plus.

When a text originates in the language of a majority of its intended readers, that language communicates with special clarity. In chapter nine on the Holy Spirit, for instance, the cultural application is headed "The Spirit Is the Immediacy of God." This eloquent phrase communicates well to U.S. readers accustomed to instant access and rapid response. It situates the truth of the Holy Spirit's activity in the English-speaking experience.

*The **U.S. Catholic Catechism** situates the truths of faith in a context particular to our nation*. Here, for instance, the new *Catechism* has some comments on New Age spirituality under the first commandment—not much, but more than the universal *Catechism*. It has more content on abortion and introduces such topics as abuse, charismatic renewal, civil disobedience, computers (including the Internet and software piracy), copyright violations (under the seventh commandment) and fertility ("fecundity" in the universal *Catechism*) in the index.

The U.S. bishops have included excerpts from teaching documents they've issued in the past, such as a response to the events of September 11 and reflections on the themes of the Church's social teaching. By reiterating them in the *U.S. Catechism*, they underline their importance and teach by their very placement within the text.

How Can This Catechism Affect Your Life?

The *U.S. Catholic Catechism for Adults* is exactly that: Catholic and for adults. It can be used confidently as a resource for every Catholic. It could be a reference for the family, but it is clearly meant to be more than that.

In addition to the stories, the cultural segments, and the prayerful conclusions to every chapter, the interested reader will find questions and answers, key doctrinal statements for easy perusal, and discussion questions that could engage many a study group and any creative, curious, concerned Catholic.

This catechism should be a staple of the RCIA, both for its teaching team and for inquirers. It is a stimulating resource for parish study groups, who may choose to focus on the discussion questions.

Chapter eight, "The Saving Death and Resurrection of Christ," poses these questions: "How would you help people come to faith in the resurrection of Christ? Why is it so central to your faith?" You'll find pointers to these and many other questions about the Catholic faith in the *U.S. Catholic Catechism for Adults*.

Questions for Reflection

1. Why is the distinction between a universal catechism and a local catechism important?
2. Why is it significant that the United States catechism is specifically "for adults"? What might this say about our need to learn about our faith throughout our lives?

Conclusion

Any and every human attempt to express in words God's self-revelation and our response to that revelation is bound to have imperfections and deficiencies, for the reality of God is too great for us ever to comprehend, much less to commit to writing. There is always more to learn. This means that there will always be positions once taken that have to be revised—even changed—in the light of further understandings of the truth.

In John's Gospel Jesus promises his followers: "When the Spirit of Truth comes, he will guide you into all the truth" (John 16:13)—but he does not say "all at once." As Vatican II's Constitution on Divine Revelation tells us: "God, who spoke of old, still maintains an uninterrupted conversation with the bride of his beloved Son" (8). This ongoing "conversation" of God with the Church influences the way the Church writes catechisms and other documents.

Does this mean that all catechisms are provisional documents that will always change with time? This cannot be answered with a simple yes or no. It must be firmly stated that there is nothing provisional about the substance of the Catholic faith. Yet it must also be said, with equal firmness, that this substance will not always be expressed in the same way or even with the same clarity in different ages of the Church's history. Pope John XXIII, in his speech opening the Second Vatican Council, made this point very forcefully: "The substance of the ancient deposit of faith is one thing; the way it is presented is another."

A catechism that comes to us from the magisterium of the Church will express the authentic teaching of the Church in accordance with the best understanding and conscience that the magisterium has at the time the catechism is produced. We who live in the twenty-first century are able to say that, while the basic substance of the faith is essentially the same in the *Roman Catechism* of the Council of Trent and the *Catechism of the Catholic Church*, the way in which that substance is expressed in these two documents differs considerably. Both reflect the times in which they were written. Most Catholics today will find the language of the new catechism more congenial to them than the text of the *Roman Catechism*. The Tridentine catechism rose out of religious controversies that today are in large part foreign to us. The more ecumenical thrust of the new *Catechism* much better suits our present religious outlook.

Perhaps the most striking contrast between these two catechisms would be part two in each of them, namely, the section that deals with the sacraments. Trent's catechism shows its indebtedness to the scholasticism that was the theological environment of the day. Thus, it presents the sacraments in terms of signs, matter, and form, cause and effect, and so on. The *Catechism of the Catholic Church* begins its presentation with a fine study of liturgy and our participation in the celebration of the Christian mystery. It clearly reveals the influence of the twentieth-century liturgical movement and Vatican II's Constitution on the Sacred Liturgy.

The *Catechism*'s emphasis on the social teachings of the Church and its linking of the Eucharist with concern for the poor is new. This is understandable: Those who wrote the *Roman Catechism* could not have known of the coming Industrial Revolution, the social ills it would breed, and the Church's consequent obligation to speak out against the inhumanities that a technological society would visit on so many people.

Many other examples of differences could be mentioned. Let one more issue—a highly emotional one—suffice: namely, the fate of children who die without baptism. The Tridentine catechism was adamant: "Infants, unless baptized, cannot enter heaven." The new *Catechism* speaks much more compassionately, saying that the Church simply entrusts children who have died without baptism to the mercy of God. The divine mercy and Jesus's tenderness toward children allow us to hope that there is a way of salvation for such children (see 1261).

The Catholic faith does not change, but we are always learning anew how to practice it within the times, cultures, and challenges we face. The *Catechism of the Catholic Church* is one more way we can grow in our understanding of the faith.

Sources

Catechism of the Catholic Church, second edition (Washington, D.C.: USCCB, 1994).

McBride, Alfred, O.Praem. "A Walk Through the New Catechism," *Catholic Update,* August 1994.

Morrow, Carol Ann. "A Quick Look at the New U.S. Catechism," *Catholic Update,* September 2006.

Shannon, William H. *Exploring the Catechism of the Catholic Church* (Cincinnati: St. Anthony Messenger Press, 1995).

Contributors

Alfred McBride, O. PRAEM., holds a diploma in catechetics from Lumen Vitae, Brussels, and a doctorate in religious education from the Catholic University of America, Washington, D.C. His books include *The Challenge of the Cross: Praying the Stations*; *Staying Faithful Today: To God, Ourselves, One Another*; *A Short History of the Mass*; *The Story of the Church*; and *A Priest Forever: Nine Signs of Renewal and Hope*.

Carol Ann Morrow, a widely published author and editor, produced the audio edition of the *U.S. Catholic Catechism for Adults,* available from Franciscan Media.

William H. Shannon was the founding president of the International Thomas Merton Society and the author of numerous *Catholic Update* newsletters, *Thomas Merton: An Introduction,* and *Exploring the Catechism of the Catholic Church*.